BIBLE PUZZLES
MATCH-IT

Publisher ....*Arthur L. Miley*

Authors ....*Roy J. Nichols*
Monte Corley

Art Director ....*Debbie Birch*

Cover Design ....*Gary Zupkas*

Production Director ....*Barbara Bucher*

Production Artist ....*Nelson Beltran*

Proofreader ....*Barbara Bucher*

Rainbow Publishers
Copyright © 1998 • Tenth Printing
Rainbow Books • P.O. Box 261129 • San Diego, CA 92196

#RB36154
ISBN 0-937282-54-5

BIBLE PUZZLES
MATCH-IT

CONTENTS

INTRODUCTION

The exciting puzzles contained in this *Bible Puzzles* book will bring new fun and enthusiasm to the learning and reviewing of Bible facts and the development of Bible-use skills. The individual puzzle sheets can be used for readiness, reinforcement and review activities, and for enrichment in the Bible class and at home.

Each of the four books in the *Bible Puzzles* series provides a variety of puzzles for children ages 8 through 13 (but older teens and adults will enjoy many of the puzzles too!). Individual puzzles may be duplicated for use with groups. Answers are provided on the back of each puzzle.

The King James Version of the Bible is the biblical reference for the puzzles.

1
MATCH-IT
PUZZLES

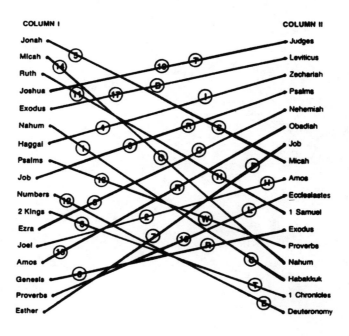

PEOPLE AND EVENTS

Below are two columns. Match the hero and the deed by writing the number of the person in the space before the event.

HEROES	DEEDS
1. Samson	_____ denied he knew Christ.
2. David	_____ killed Sisera with a tent peg.
3. Joshua	_____ slew a giant enemy.
4. Jael	_____ refused to bow down to the gods of Nebuchadnezzar.
5. Moses	_____ was cast into a den of lions.
6. Rahab	_____ pulled down a building.
7. Shadrach, Meshach, Abednego	_____ hid the spies of Israel.
8. Esther	_____ was the first Christian martyr.
9. Paul	_____ fought against the Midianites.
10. Gideon	_____ led Israel against Jericho.
11. Stephen	_____ commanded Pharaoh to let Israel go.
12. Nehemiah	_____ saved her people.
13. Peter	_____ built a boat to save his family.
14. Daniel	_____ helped rebuild the walls of Jerusalem.
15. Noah	_____ preached the Gospel while in prison.

PEOPLE AND EVENTS

Below are two columns. Match the hero and the deed by writing the number of the person in the space before the event.

HEROES	DEEDS
1. Samson	13 denied he knew Christ.
2. David	4 killed Sisera with a tent peg.
3. Joshua	2 slew a giant enemy.
4. Jael	7 refused to bow down to the gods of Nebuchadnezzar.
5. Moses	14 was cast into a den of lions.
6. Rahab	1 pulled down a building.
7. Shadrach, Meshach, Abednego	6 hid the spies of Israel.
8. Esther	11 was the first Christian martyr.
9. Paul	10 fought against the Midianites.
10. Gideon	3 led Israel against Jericho.
11. Stephen	5 commanded Pharaoh to let Israel go.
12. Nehemiah	8 saved her people.
13. Peter	15 built a boat to save his family.
14. Daniel	12 helped rebuild the walls of Jerusalem.
15. Noah	9 preached the Gospel while in prison.

PEOPLE AND THINGS

Match the people in COLUMN I to the object or place in COLUMN II with which they are associated. Write the number of the person in the space before the correct thing. If you need help, refer to the Scriptures listed.

COLUMN I	COLUMN II
1. Noah	____ Ladder (Gen. 28:10-12)
2. Eve	____ Ark (Gen. 6:13-14)
3. Cain	____ Ravens (1 Kings 17:1-4)
4. Joseph	____ Altar (Gen. 22:9)
5. David	____ Fish (Jonah 1:17)
6. Rahab	____ Locusts & Wild Honey (Matt. 3:4)
7. Isaac	____ Calf (Exod. 32:3-4)
8. Daniel	____ Venison (Gen. 27:5)
9. Shadrach	____ Hair (Judg. 16:13)
10. Moses	____ Fruit (Gen. 3:2)
11. Jonah	____ Pitchers (Judg. 7:19)
12. Samson	____ Cross (Matt. 27:22-23)
13. Jesus	____ Coat (Gen. 37:3)
14. Judas	____ Lions (Dan. 6:16)
15. Naaman	____ Jordan River (2 Kings 5:9-14)
16. Israelites	____ 30 Pieces of Silver (Matt. 27:3)
17. Lot's wife	____ Sycamore Tree (Luke 19:2-4)
18. John the Baptist	____ Sling (1 Sam. 17:39-40)
19. Aaron	____ Manna (Exod. 16:15)
20. Jacob	____ Cord (Josh. 2:3-18)
21. Gideon	____ Fire (Dan. 3:20)
22. Elijah	____ Salt (Gen. 19:23-26)
23. Zaccheus	____ Mount Sinai (Exod. 24:16-18)
24. Esau	____ Fruit of the ground (Gen. 4:3)

PEOPLE AND THINGS

Match the people in COLUMN I to the object or place in COLUMN II with which they are associated. Write the number of the person in the space before the correct thing. If you need help, refer to the Scriptures listed.

COLUMN I		COLUMN II
1. Noah	20	Ladder (Gen. 28:10-12)
2. Eve	1	Ark (Gen. 6:13-14)
3. Cain	22	Ravens (1 Kings 17:1-4)
4. Joseph	7	Altar (Gen. 22:9)
5. David	11	Fish (Jonah 1:17)
6. Rahab	18	Locusts & Wild Honey (Matt. 3:4)
7. Isaac	19	Calf (Exod. 32:3-4)
8. Daniel	24	Venison (Gen. 27:5)
9. Shadrach	12	Hair (Judg. 16:13)
10. Moses	2	Fruit (Gen. 3:2)
11. Jonah	21	Pitchers (Judg. 7:19)
12. Samson	13	Cross (Matt. 27:22-23)
13. Jesus	4	Coat (Gen. 37:3)
14. Judas	8	Lions (Dan. 6:16)
15. Naaman	15	Jordan River (2 Kings 5:9-14)
16. Israelites	14	30 Pieces of Silver (Matt. 27:3)
17. Lot's wife	23	Sycamore Tree (Luke 19:2-4)
18. John the Baptist	5	Sling (1 Sam. 17:39-40)
19. Aaron	16	Manna (Exod. 16:15)
20. Jacob	6	Cord (Josh. 2:3-18)
21. Gideon	9	Fire (Dan. 3:20)
22. Elijah	17	Salt (Gen. 19:23-26)
23. Zaccheus	10	Mount Sinai (Exod. 24:16-18)
24. Esau	3	Fruit of the ground (Gen. 4:3)

PEOPLE AND PLACES

Below are two columns. Match the person and the place by writing the number of the person in the space before the place. If you need help, refer to the Scripture after the place listing.

PEOPLE	PLACES
1. Joseph	____ Gath (1 Sam. 17:4)
2. Joshua	____ Bethany (John 12:1)
3. Abram	____ Egypt (Gen. 39:1)
4. Adam	____ Thyatira (Acts 16:14)
5. Moses	____ Jericho (Josh. 6:1-2)
6. Jesus	____ Caesarea (Acts 10:1)
7. Paul (Saul)	____ Mount Carmel (1 Kings 18:20-21)
8. Lot	____ Moab (Ruth 1:1-4)
9. Peter	____ Ur (Gen. 15:1-7)
10. Lydia	____ Sodom (Gen. 13:12)
11. Lazarus	____ Jericho (Josh. 2:1)
12. Elijah	____ Ararat (Gen. 8:1-4)
13. David	____ Midian (Judg. 7:7-8)
14. Cornelius	____ Eden (Gen. 2:7-8)
15. Philip	____ Damascus (Acts 9:8)
16. Nebuchadnezzar	____ Jerusalem (Acts 2:14)
17. Noah	____ Babylon (Dan. 1:1)
18. Cain	____ Sinai (Exod. 19:20)
19. Gideon	____ Nazareth (Luke 4:14-16)
20. Goliath	____ Gaza (Acts 8:26)
21. Barnabas	____ Bethlehem (1 Sam. 17:12)
22. Rahab	____ Antioch (Acts 11:22)
23. Sarah	____ Nod (Gen. 4:16)
24. Demetrius	____ Ephesus (Acts 19:24-26)
25. Ruth	____ Kirjatharba (Gen. 23:2)

PEOPLE AND PLACES

Below are two columns. Match the person and the place by writing the number of the person in the space before the place. If you need help, refer to the Scripture after the place listing.

PEOPLE	PLACES
1. Joseph	20 Gath (1 Sam. 17:4)
2. Joshua	11 Bethany (John 12:1)
3. Abram	1 Egypt (Gen. 39:1)
4. Adam	10 Thyatira (Acts 16:14)
5. Moses	2 Jericho (Josh. 6:1-2)
6. Jesus	14 Caesarea (Acts 10:1)
7. Paul (Saul)	12 Mount Carmel (1 Kings 18:20-21)
8. Lot	25 Moab (Ruth 1:1-4)
9. Peter	3 Ur (Gen. 15:1-7)
10. Lydia	8 Sodom (Gen. 13:12)
11. Lazarus	22 Jericho (Josh. 2:1)
12. Elijah	17 Ararat (Gen. 8:1-4)
13. David	19 Midian (Judg. 7:7-8)
14. Cornelius	4 Eden (Gen. 2:7-8)
15. Philip	7 Damascus (Acts 9:8)
16. Nebuchadnezzar	9 Jerusalem (Acts 2:14)
17. Noah	16 Babylon (Dan. 1:1)
18. Cain	5 Sinai (Exod. 19:20)
19. Gideon	6 Nazareth (Luke 4:14-16)
20. Goliath	15 Gaza (Acts 8:26)
21. Barnabas	13 Bethlehem (1 Sam. 17:12)
22. Rahab	21 Antioch (Acts 11:22)
23. Sarah	18 Nod (Gen. 4:16)
24. Demetrius	24 Ephesus (Acts 19:24-26)
25. Ruth	23 Kirjatharba (Gen. 23:2)

PEOPLE AND BOOKS

Match the Old Testament characters to the Bible book in which they are first found. Place the number for each name in the space before the correct Bible book. You may use a concordance or Bible dictionary if you need help.

COLUMN I	COLUMN II
1. Adam	____ Genesis
2. Cain	____ 1 Samuel
3. Noah	____ Daniel
4. Naaman	____ Genesis
5. Abram	____ 1 Samuel
6. Elijah	____ Genesis
7. Isaac	____ Joshua
8. Rahab	____ Genesis
9. Sarah	____ Genesis
10. Jezebel	____ 1 Kings
11. Jacob	____ Genesis
12. Shadrach	____ Jonah
13. Esau	____ Genesis
14. Ruth	____ Judges
15. Joseph	____ Genesis
16. Samson	____ 1 Kings
17. David	____ Judges
18. Moses	____ Ruth
19. Saul	____ Daniel
20. Gideon	____ 2 Kings
21. Daniel	____ Exodus
22. Jonah	____ Genesis

PEOPLE AND BOOKS

Match the Old Testament characters to the Bible book in which they are first found. Place the number for each name in the space before the correct Bible book. You may use a concordance or Bible dictionary if you need help.

COLUMN I	COLUMN II
1. Adam	_1_ Genesis
2. Cain	_17_ 1 Samuel
3. Noah	_12_ Daniel
4. Naaman	_2_ Genesis
5. Abram	_19_ 1 Samuel
6. Elijah	_3_ Genesis
7. Isaac	_8_ Joshua
8. Rahab	_5_ Genesis
9. Sarah	_7_ Genesis
10. Jezebel	_6_ 1 Kings
11. Jacob	_9_ Genesis
12. Shadrach	_22_ Jonah
13. Esau	_11_ Genesis
14. Ruth	_16_ Judges
15. Joseph	_13_ Genesis
16. Samson	_10_ 1 Kings
17. David	_20_ Judges
18. Moses	_14_ Ruth
19. Saul	_21_ Daniel
20. Gideon	_4_ 2 Kings
21. Daniel	_18_ Exodus
22. Jonah	_15_ Genesis

FATHERS AND SONS

Try to match the fathers in the list below with their sons at right. If you need help, refer to the Scripture after the son's name.

FATHERS

1. Adam	9. Reuben
2. Noah	10. Joseph
3. Seth	11. Moses
4. Cain	12. Kish
5. Abraham	13. Jesse
6. Isaac	14. Saul
7. Jacob	15. David
8. Judah	16. Solomon
	17. Herod

18. Zebedee
19. Zacharias
20. Enoch
21. Lamech
22. Terah
23. Haran
24. Israel
25. God

SONS

_____ Jesus (Matt. 3:16-17)

_____ Lot (Gen. 11:31)

_____ Absalom (2 Sam. 13:1)

_____ Shem (Gen. 6:10)

_____ Methuselah (Gen. 5:21)

_____ Jacob (Gen. 25:26)

_____ Hanoch (Gen. 46:9)

_____ Abram (Gen. 11:31)

_____ Enos (Gen. 5:7)

_____ Seth (Gen. 5:3)

_____ Enoch (Gen. 4:17)

_____ Noah (Gen. 5:30)

_____ John (Luke 1:13)

_____ Er (Gen. 38:2-3)

_____ Joseph (Gen. 37:3)

_____ Isaac (Gen. 21:5)

_____ James (Mark 1:19)

_____ Rehoboam (1 Kings 11:43)

_____ Reuben (Gen. 35:23)

_____ Manasseh (Gen. 46:20)

_____ Gershom (Ex. 2:21-22)

_____ Saul (1 Sam. 9:1-2)

_____ David (1 Sam. 16:19)

_____ Archelaus (Matt. 2:22)

_____ Jonathan (1 Sam. 13:16)

FATHERS AND SONS

SONS

Try to match the fathers in the list below with their sons at right. If you need help, refer to the Scripture after the son's name.

_8_ Er (Gen. 38:2-3)

_24_ Joseph (Gen. 37:3)

_5_ Isaac (Gen. 21:5)

_18_ James (Mark 1:19)

_16_ Rehoboam (1 Kings 11:43)

_7_ Reuben (Gen. 35:23)

_10_ Manasseh (Gen. 46:20)

_11_ Gershom (Ex. 2:21-22)

_12_ Saul (1 Sam. 9:1-2)

_13_ David (1 Sam. 16:19)

_17_ Archelaus (Matt. 2:22)

_14_ Jonathan (1 Sam. 13:16)

_25_ Jesus (Matt. 3:16-17)

_23_ Lot (Gen. 11:31)

_15_ Absalom (2 Sam. 13:1)

_2_ Shem (Gen. 6:10)

_20_ Methuselah (Gen. 5:21)

_6_ Jacob (Gen. 25:26)

_9_ Hanoch (Gen. 46:9)

_22_ Abram (Gen. 11:31)

_3_ Enos (Gen. 5:7)

_1_ Seth (Gen. 5:3)

_4_ Enoch (Gen. 4:17)

_21_ Noah (Gen. 5:30)

_19_ John (Luke 1:13)

FATHERS

1. Adam	9. Reuben
2. Noah	10. Joseph
3. Seth	11. Moses
4. Cain	12. Kish
5. Abraham	13. Jesse
6. Isaac	14. Saul
7. Jacob	15. David
8. Judah	16. Solomon
18. Zebedee	17. Herod
19. Zacharias	
20. Enoch	
21. Lamech	
22. Terah	
23. Haran	
24. Israel	
25. God	

SCRIPTURE AND VERSE

Match the Bible verse on the left with its Scripture reference on the right by placing its number in the correct blank.

1. "In the beginning God created the heaven and the earth."

       _____ Galatians 5:22-23

2. "For God so loved the world, that he gave His only begotten Son, that whosoever believeth in Him should not perish, but have everlasting life.

       _____ John 11:35

3. "Jesus wept."

       _____ Mark 16:15

4. "For unto you is born this day in the city of David a Saviour, which is Christ the Lord."

       _____ Hebrews 11:1

5. "And he said unto them, Go ye into all the world, and preach the Gospel to every creature."

       _____ Genesis 1:1

6. "Now faith is the substance of things hoped for, the evidence of things not seen."

       _____ Luke 2:11

7. "And the Holy Ghost descended in a bodily shape like a dove upon Him, and a voice came from heaven, which said, Thou art My beloved Son; in thee I am well pleased."

       _____ John 3:16

8. "But the fruit of the Spirit is love, joy, peace, longsuffering, gentleness, goodness, faith, meekness, temperance: against such there is no law."

       _____ Acts 2:38

9. "Pray without ceasing."

       _____ 1 Thessalonians 5:17

10. "Then Peter said unto them, Repent, and be baptized every one of you in the name of Jesus Christ for the remission of sins, and ye shall receive the gift of the Holy Ghost."

       _____ Luke 3:22

SCRIPTURE AND VERSE

Match the Bible verse on the left with its Scripture reference on the right by placing its number in the correct blank.

1. "In the beginning God created the heaven and the earth."

<u>8</u> Galatians 5:22-23

2. "For God so loved the world, that he gave His only begotten Son, that whosoever believeth in Him should not perish, but have everlasting life.

<u>3</u> John 11:35

3. "Jesus wept."

<u>5</u> Mark 16:15

4. "For unto you is born this day in the city of David a Saviour, which is Christ the Lord."

<u>6</u> Hebrews 11:1

5. "And he said unto them, Go ye into all the world, and preach the Gospel to every creature."

<u>1</u> Genesis 1:1

6. "Now faith is the substance of things hoped for, the evidence of things not seen."

<u>4</u> Luke 2:11

7. "And the Holy Ghost descended in a bodily shape like a dove upon Him, and a voice came from heaven, which said, Thou art My beloved Son; in thee I am well pleased."

<u>2</u> John 3:16

8. "But the fruit of the Spirit is love, joy, peace, longsuffering, gentleness, goodness, faith, meekness, temperance: against such there is no law."

<u>10</u> Acts 2:38

9. "Pray without ceasing."

<u>9</u> 1 Thessalonians 5:17

10. "Then Peter said unto them, Repent, and be baptized every one of you in the name of Jesus Christ for the remission of sins, and ye shall receive the gift of the Holy Ghost."

<u>7</u> Luke 3:22

OLD TESTAMENT LINE-UP

Draw a straight line from the book in Column I to the one that follows it in Column II. The line will pass through a number and a letter. The number tells you where to put the letter below. Then read the message in the boxes.

COLUMN I

Jonah •

Micah •

Ruth •

Joshua •

Exodus •

Nahum •

Haggai •

Psalms •

Job •

Numbers •

2 Kings •

Ezra •

Joel •

Amos •

Genesis •

Proverbs •

Esther •

COLUMN II

• Judges

• Leviticus

• Zechariah

• Psalms

• Nehemiah

• Obadiah

• Job

• Micah

• Amos

• Ecclesiastes

• 1 Samuel

• Exodus

• Proverbs

• Nahum

• Habakkuk

• 1 Chronicles

• Deuteronomy

(5) (14) (10) (T) (11) (17) (D) (I) (4) (R) (S) (1) (9) (O) (O) (F) (13) (H) (H) (R) (12) (8) (L) (2) (W) (6) (7) (16) (R) (15) (C) (3) (T) (E)

1	2	3	4	5	6	7	8	9	10	11	12	13	14	15	16	17

OLD TESTAMENT LINE-UP

Draw a straight line from the book in Column I to the one that follows it in Column II. The line will pass through a number and a letter. The number tells you where to put the letter below. Then read the message in the boxes.

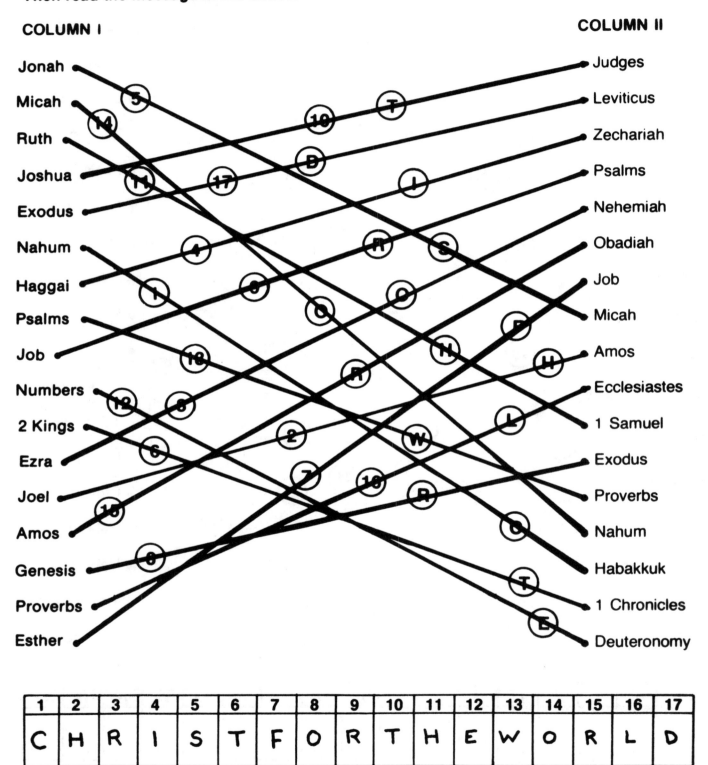

COLUMN I

Jonah
Micah
Ruth
Joshua
Exodus
Nahum
Haggai
Psalms
Job
Numbers
2 Kings
Ezra
Joel
Amos
Genesis
Proverbs
Esther

COLUMN II

Judges
Leviticus
Zechariah
Psalms
Nehemiah
Obadiah
Job
Micah
Amos
Ecclesiastes
1 Samuel
Exodus
Proverbs
Nahum
Habakkuk
1 Chronicles
Deuteronomy

1	2	3	4	5	6	7	8	9	10	11	12	13	14	15	16	17
C	H	R	I	S	T	F	O	R	T	H	E	W	O	R	L	D

NEW TESTAMENT LINE-UP

Connect each book in Column I with the one that follows it in Column II. The straight line will pass through a number and a letter. The number tells you where to put the letter below. The letters in the boxes will spell out a message.

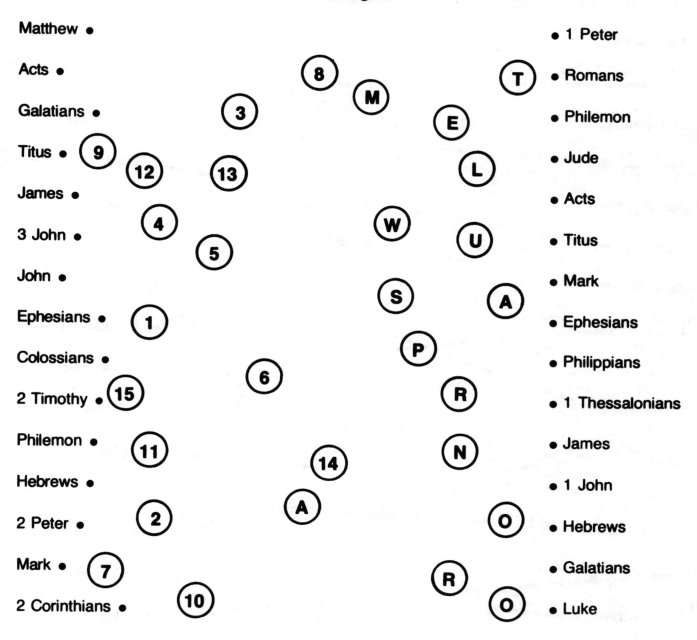

1	2	3	4	5	6	7	8	9	10	11	12	13	14	15

NEW TESTAMENT LINE-UP

Connect each book in Column I with the one that follows it in Column II. The straight line will pass through a number and a letter. The number tells you where to put the letter below. The letters in the boxes will spell out a message.

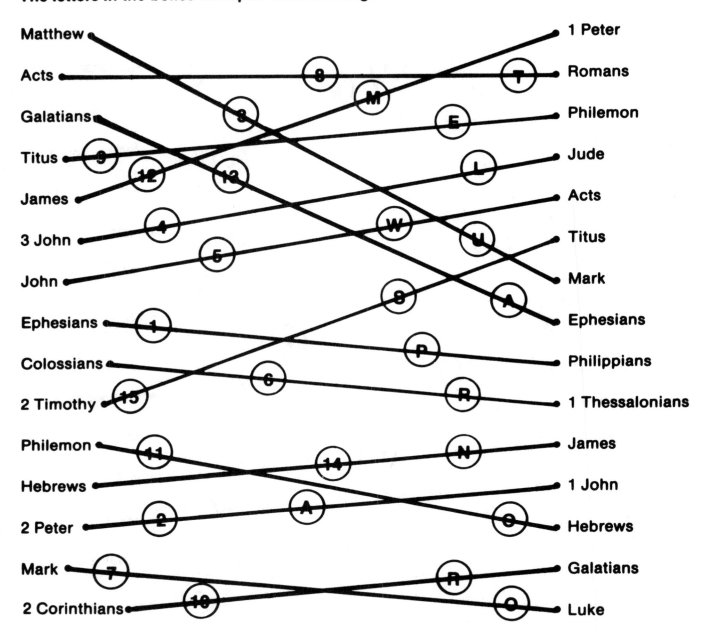

1	2	3	4	5	6	7	8	9	10	11	12	13	14	15
P	A	U	L	W	R	O	T	E	R	O	M	A	N	S

OLD TESTAMENT LETTER MATCH

Figure out what the letter is. Then put it in the box below the sentence number.

1. The 2nd letter in the name of the 20th book

2. The 6th letter in the name of the 22nd book

3. The 3rd letter in the name of the 39th book

4. The 11th letter in the name of the 5th book

5. The 3rd letter in the name of the 15th book

6. The 1st letter in the name of the 26th book

7. The 4th letter in the name of the 3rd book

8. The 2nd letter in the name of the 6th book

9. The 1st letter in the name of the 30th book

10. The 2nd letter in the name of the 18th book

11. The 5th letter in the name of the 7th book

12. The 4th letter in the name of the 34th book

13. The 1st letter in the name of the 27th book

14. The 3rd letter in the name of the 24th book

15. The 6th letter in the name of the 22nd book

5	11	9	13	2	10	14	4	8	12	1	3	7	15	6

OLD TESTAMENT LETTER MATCH

Figure out what the letter is. Then put it in the box below the sentence number.

1. The 2nd letter in the name of the 20th book

2. The 6th letter in the name of the 22nd book

3. The 3rd letter in the name of the 39th book

4. The 11th letter in the name of the 5th book

5. The 3rd letter in the name of the 15th book

6. The 1st letter in the name of the 26th book

7. The 4th letter in the name of the 3rd book

8. The 2nd letter in the name of the 6th book

9. The 1st letter in the name of the 30th book

10. The 2nd letter in the name of the 18th book

11. The 5th letter in the name of the 7th book

12. The 4th letter in the name of the 34th book

13. The 1st letter in the name of the 27th book

14. The 3rd letter in the name of the 24th book

15. The 6th letter in the name of the 22nd book

5	11	9	13	2	10	14	4	8	12	1	3	7	15	6
R	E	A	D	F	O	R	Y	O	U	R	L	I	F	E

NEW TESTAMENT LETTER MATCH

Figure out what the letter is. Then put it in the box below the sentence number.

1. The 3rd letter in the name of the 1st book

2. The 2nd letter in the name of the 13th book

3. The 1st letter in the name of the 10th book

4. The 1st letter in the name of the 9th book

5. The 4th letter in the name of the 15th book

6. The 4th letter in the name of the 5th book

7. The 1st letter in the name of the 11th book

8. The 4th letter in the name of the 3rd book

9. The 4th letter in the name of the 18th book

10. The 2nd letter in the name of the 16th book

11. The 6th letter in the name of the 6th book

12. The 1st letter in the name of the 9th book

13. The 2nd letter in the name of the 4th book

14. The 9th letter in the name of the 27th book

15. The 3rd letter in the name of the 26th book

16. The 9th letter in the name of the 12th book

17. The 4th letter in the name of the 20th book

18. The 6th letter in the name of the 19th book

19. The 5th letter in the name of the 17th book

1	2	3	4	5	6	7	8	9	10	11	12	13	14	15	16	17	18	19

NEW TESTAMENT LETTER MATCH

Figure out what the letter is. Then put it in the box below the sentence number.

1. The 3rd letter in the name of the 1st book

2. The 2nd letter in the name of the 13th book

3. The 1st letter in the name of the 10th book

4. The 1st letter in the name of the 9th book

5. The 4th letter in the name of the 15th book

6. The 4th letter in the name of the 5th book

7. The 1st letter in the name of the 11th book

8. The 4th letter in the name of the 3rd book

9. The 4th letter in the name of the 18th book

10. The 2nd letter in the name of the 16th book

11. The 6th letter in the name of the 6th book

12. The 1st letter in the name of the 9th book

13. The 2nd letter in the name of the 4th book

14. The 9th letter in the name of the 27th book

15. The 3rd letter in the name of the 26th book

16. The 9th letter in the name of the 12th book

17. The 4th letter in the name of the 20th book

18. The 6th letter in the name of the 19th book

19. The 5th letter in the name of the 17th book

1	2	3	4	5	6	7	8	9	10	11	12	13	14	15	16	17	18	19
T	H	E	G	O	S	P	E	L	I	S	G	O	O	D	N	E	W	S

BIBLE MATCH-UP

Match the person in Column I with the person, place, event or object associated with him or her. If you need help, you may look up the Scriptures listed.

COLUMN I

1. Joseph
2. Lydia
3. Saul
4. Shem
5. Mary Magdalene
6. John
7. Daniel
8. Herod
9. Eve
10. Uzza
11. Jael
12. Judas
13. Aaron
14. Hannah
15. Dorcas
16. Salome
17. Nathanael
18. Esau
19. Mary of Bethany
20. Solomon

COLUMN 2

a. _____ Great Flood (Genesis 7:10-13)

b. _____ Ark of God (I Chronicles 13:5-10)

c. _____ Tree of the Knowledge of Good and Evil (Gen. 2:17, 3:1-6)

d. _____ Tent nail (peg) (Judges 4:17-24)

e. _____ Wisdom (I Kings 4:29-34)

f. _____ Jesus saw him under a fig tree (John 1:47-49)

g. _____ Famine (Genesis 41:25-41)

h. _____ Lion's Den (Daniel 6:16-23)

i. _____ Seller of purple (Acts 16:14)

j. _____ Martha (John 11:1, 2)

k. _____ Road to Damascus (Acts 9:1-8)

l. _____ Prayer for a son (I Samuel 1:9-11; 27)

m. _____ Went to Jesus' sepulcher with the two Marys (Mark 16:1, 2)

n. _____ Jacob's twin brother (Genesis 25:25)

o. _____ Slaughter of young children (Matthew 2:16)

p. _____ Isle of Patmos (Revelation 1:9)

q. _____ 30 pieces of silver (Matthew 26:14-16)

r. _____ Healed of seven demons (Luke 8:2)

s. _____ Raised from the dead (Acts 9:36-42)

t. _____ Golden calf (Exodus 32:1-24)

BIBLE MATCH-UP

Match the person in Column I with the person, place, event or object associated with him or her. If you need help, you may look up the Scriptures listed.

COLUMN I		COLUMN 2
1. Joseph	a. __4__	Great Flood (Genesis 7:10-13)
2. Lydia	b. __10__	Ark of God (I Chronicles 13:5-10)
3. Saul	c. __9__	Tree of the Knowledge of Good and Evil (Gen. 2:17, 3:1-6)
4. Shem	d. __11__	Tent nail (peg) (Judges 4:17-24)
5. Mary Magdalene	e. __20__	Wisdom (I Kings 4:29-34)
6. John	f. __17__	Jesus saw him under a fig tree (John 1:47-49)
7. Daniel	g. __1__	Famine (Genesis 41:25-41)
8. Herod	h. __7__	Lion's Den (Daniel 6:16-23)
9. Eve	i. __2__	Seller of purple (Acts 16:14)
10. Uzza	j. __19__	Martha (John 11:1, 2)
11. Jael	k. __3__	Road to Damascus (Acts 9:1-8)
12. Judas	l. __14__	Prayer for a son (I Samuel 1:9-11; 27)
13. Aaron	m. __16__	Went to Jesus' sepulcher with the two Marys (Mark 16:1, 2)
14. Hannah	n. __18__	Jacob's twin brother (Genesis 25:25)
15. Dorcas	o. __8__	Slaughter of young children (Matthew 2:16)
16. Salome	p. __6__	Isle of Patmos (Revelation 1:9)
17. Nathanael	q. __12__	30 pieces of silver (Matthew 26:14-16)
18. Esau	r. __5__	Healed of seven demons (Luke 8:2)
19. Mary of Bethany	s. __15__	Raised from the dead (Acts 9:36-42)
20. Solomon	t. __13__	Golden calf (Exodus 32:1-24)

2
CATEGORY PUZZLES

Scripture	Person	Place	Event
2 Kings 17:1-6	4	4	6
1 Samuel 10:17-24	14	12	5
1 Kings 8:1-21	10	9/11	13
1 Samuel 16:4-13	7	2	1
2 Kings 18:1-5	3	1/14	7
2 Kings 24:10-16	13	9/11	3
1 Samuel 13:7-14	1	5	4
1 Kings 16:29-32	5	6	10
1 Samuel 17:19-51	12	8	2
2 Kings 5:1-14	2	10	12
2 Kings 22:1–23:5	8	1/14	9
1 Kings 17:8-16	9	3	11
1 Kings 22:29-41	6	7	8
1 Kings 11:43-12:1	11	13	14

PERSON, PLACE, OR THING?

Listed below are 30 words from the Bible. Each one belongs to one of the categories below. Write each word in the proper column. If you don't know one, you may look up its Scripture or find it in a Bible dictionary.

1. Coulter (1 Sam. 13:20)
2. Bahurim (2 Sam. 17:18)
3. Baasha (1 Kings 15:27)
4. Awl (Exod. 21:6)
5. Chalcedony (Rev. 21:19)
6. Farthing (Matt. 10:29)
7. Cassia (Exod. 30:24)
8. Artaxerxes (Ezra 7:1)
9. Timnath (Judg. 14:1)
10. Goad (1 Sam. 13:21)
11. Bekah (Exod. 38:26)
12. Cockatrice (Isa. 14:29)
13. Cummin (Isa. 28:24-27)
14. Ephod (Exod. 28:4)
15. Mitre (Exod. 29:6)
16. Calamus (Exod. 30:23)
17. Harrow (2 Sam. 12:31)
18. Cankerworm (Joel 1:4)
19. Publican (Matt. 10:3)
20. Ferret (Lev. 11:30)
21. Carbuncle (Exod. 28:17)
22. Kine (Gen. 32:15)
23. Carchemish (2 Chron. 35:20)
24. Vesture (Gen. 41:42)
25. Chrysoprasus (Rev. 21:20)
26. Whelp (Gen. 49:9)
27. Kirjathjearim (1 Sam. 7:1)
28. Galbanum (Exod. 30:34)
29. Onycha (Exod. 30:34)
30. Shekel (Exod. 30:13)

Clothing	Places	Spices	Animals

Tools	Persons	Minerals	Money

PERSON, PLACE, OR THING?

Listed below are 30 words from the Bible. Each one belongs to one of the categories below. Write each word in the proper column. If you don't know one, you may look up its Scripture or find it in a Bible dictionary.

1. Coulter (1 Sam. 13:20)
2. Bahurim (2 Sam. 17:18)
3. Baasha (1 Kings 15:27)
4. Awl (Exod. 21:6)
5. Chalcedony (Rev. 21:19)
6. Farthing (Matt. 10:29)
7. Cassia (Exod. 30:24)
8. Artaxerxes (Ezra 7:1)
9. Timnath (Judg. 14:1)
10. Goad (1 Sam. 13:21)
11. Bekah (Exod. 38:26)
12. Cockatrice (Isa. 14:29)
13. Cummin (Isa. 28:24-27)
14. Ephod (Exod. 28:4)
15. Mitre (Exod. 29:6)
16. Calamus (Exod. 30:23)
17. Harrow (2 Sam. 12:31)
18. Cankerworm (Joel 1:4)
19. Publican (Matt. 10:3)
20. Ferret (Lev. 11:30)
21. Carbuncle (Exod. 28:17)
22. Kine (Gen. 32:15)
23. Carchemish (2 Chron. 35:20)
24. Vesture (Gen. 41:42)
25. Chrysoprasus (Rev. 21:20)
26. Whelp (Gen. 49:9)
27. Kirjathjearim (1 Sam. 7:1)
28. Galbanum (Exod. 30:34)
29. Onycha (Exod. 30:34)
30. Shekel (Exod. 30:13)

Clothing	Places	Spices	Animals
14	2	7	12
15	9	13	18
24	23	16	20
	27	28	22
		29	26

Tools	Persons	Minerals	Money
1	3	5	6
4	8	21	11
10	19	25	30
17			

PROPHET, PRIEST, OR KING?

Listed below are 24 names from the Bible. Write the number beside each name in the proper column below. If you don't know one, you may look up its Scripture reference.

1. Isaiah (2 Chronicles 32:20)
2. Ahab (I Kings 16:29)
3. Aaron (Exodus 30:30)
4. Eli (I Samuel 1:9)
5. Hosea (Hosea 1:1)
6. Eleazar (Numbers 26:3)
7. Jehoshaphat (I Kings 22:41)
8. Saul (I Samuel 11:15)
9. Nathan (2 Samuel 7:2)
10. Nebuchadnezzar (Daniel 3:1)
11. Zacharias (Luke 1:5)
12. Agrippa (Acts 25:13)
13. Eliashib (Nehemiah 3:1)
14. Agabus (Acts 21:10)
15. Herod (Matthew 2:1)
16. Elisha (2 Kings 3:11, 12)
17. Jehoiada (2 Kings 12:2)
18. Josiah (2 Kings 22:1)
19. Elijah (I Kings 18:22)
20. Caiaphas (John 11:49)
21. Amos (Amos 7:14, 15)
22. Hiram (I Chronicles 14:1)
23. Huldah (2 Kings 22:14)
24. Hilkiah (2 Chronicles 34:14)

PROPHET	PRIEST	KING

PROPHET, PRIEST, OR KING?

Listed below are 24 names from the Bible. Write the number beside each name in the proper column below. If you don't know one, you may look up its Scripture reference.

1. Isaiah (2 Chronicles 32:20)
2. Ahab (I Kings 16:29)
3. Aaron (Exodus 30:30)
4. Eli (I Samuel 1:9)
5. Hosea (Hosea 1:1)
6. Eleazar (Numbers 26:3)
7. Jehoshaphat (I Kings 22:41)
8. Saul (I Samuel 11:15)
9. Nathan (2 Samuel 7:2)
10. Nebuchadnezzar (Daniel 3:1)
11. Zacharias (Luke 1:5)
12. Agrippa (Acts 25:13)
13. Eliashib (Nehemiah 3:1)
14. Agabus (Acts 21:10)
15. Herod (Matthew 2:1)
16. Elisha (2 Kings 3:11, 12)
17. Jehoiada (2 Kings 12:2)
18. Josiah (2 Kings 22:1)
19. Elijah (I Kings 18:22)
20. Caiaphas (John 11:49)
21. Amos (Amos 7:14, 15)
22. Hiram (I Chronicles 14:1)
23. Huldah (2 Kings 22:14)
24. Hilkiah (2 Chronicles 34:14)

PROPHET	PRIEST	KING
1	3	2
5	4	7
9	6	8
14	11	10
16	13	12
19	17	15
21	20	18
23	24	22

ANIMAL, PLANT OR MINERAL?

Listed below are 18 words from the Bible. Each one is either a plant, animal or mineral. Write each word in the proper column below. If you don't know one, you may look up its Scripture or find it in a dictionary.

1. Juniper (Ps. 120:4)
2. Brier (Isa. 9:18)
3. Almug (1 Kings 10:11-12)
4. Ligure (Exod. 28:19)
5. Fitch (Isa. 28:25, 27)
6. Bittern (Zeph. 2:14)
7. Amethyst (Exod. 28:19)
8. Mandrake (Gen. 30: 14-16)
9. Nitre (Prov. 25:20)
10. Osprey (Lev. 11:13)
11. Dromedary (1 Kings 4:28)
12. Lign aloes (Num. 24:6)
13. Leviathan (Ps. 74:14)
14. Ossifrage (Deut. 14:12)
15. Rue (Luke 11:42)
16. Sardius (Exod. 28:17)
17. Cockatrice (Isa. 11:8)
18. Coney (Lev. 11:5)

Animal	Plant	Mineral

ANIMAL, PLANT OR MINERAL?

Listed below are 18 words from the Bible. Each one is either a plant, animal or mineral. Write each word in the proper column below. If you don't know one, you may look up its Scripture or find it in a dictionary.

1. Juniper (Ps. 120:4)
2. Brier (Isa. 9:18)
3. Almug (1 Kings 10:11-12)
4. Ligure (Exod. 28:19)
5. Fitch (Isa. 28:25, 27)
6. Bittern (Zeph. 2:14)
7. Amethyst (Exod. 28:19)
8. Mandrake (Gen. 30:14-16)
9. Nitre (Prov. 25:20)
10. Osprey (Lev. 11:13)
11. Dromedary (1 Kings 4:28)
12. Lign aloes (Num. 24:6)
13. Leviathan (Ps. 74:14)
14. Ossifrage (Deut. 14:12)
15. Rue (Luke 11:42)
16. Sardius (Exod. 28:17)
17. Cockatrice (Isa. 11:8)
18. Coney (Lev. 11:5)

Animal	Plant	Mineral
6	1	4
10	2	7
11	3	9
13	5	16
14	8	
17	12	
18	15	

GET IT TOGETHER #1

Below are four groups: Scriptures, Persons, Places, and Events. Your task is to match the person, place, and event from the list below with the passage of Scripture on the left of the chart.

Scripture	Person	Place	Event
Genesis 3			
Genesis 8			
Genesis 19			
Genesis 22			
Genesis 24			
Genesis 29			
Genesis 32			
Genesis 37			
Genesis 41			
Exodus 3			
Exodus 14			
Exodus 20			
Numbers 13			
Numbers 14			

Person	Place	Event
1. Joseph	Mt. Horeb	Sent here to find a wife for Isaac
2. Lot	Red Sea	Sentenced to wander here for forty years
3. Pharaoh	Eden	Destroyed while pursuing Israelites
4. Jacob	Sodom and Gomorrah	Offered his son in sacrifice
5. Laban	Mt. Ararat	The Ten Commandments were given
6. Servant of Abraham	Dothan	Fled destruction of wicked cities
7. Moses	The wilderness	Deceived by a serpent
8. Children of Israel	Canaan	The ark came to rest
9. Twelve spies	Mt. Sinai	Sold by brothers to Midianites
10. Abraham	Mesopotamia	Wrestled with an angel
11. Eve	Mt. Moriah	Tricked Jacob into marrying older daughter
12. Army of Egypt	Haran	Sent to "search the land" for conquest
13. Noah	Egypt	Had two dreams interpreted by Joseph
14. Moses	Peniel	Called to lead Israel out of Egypt

GET IT TOGETHER #1

Below are four groups: Scriptures, Persons, Places, and Events. Your task is to match the person, place, and event from the list below with the passage of Scripture on the left of the chart.

Scripture	Person	Place	Event
Genesis 3	11	3	7
Genesis 8	13	5	8
Genesis 19	2	4	6
Genesis 22	10	11	4
Genesis 24	6	10	1
Genesis 29	5	12	11
Genesis 32	4	14	10
Genesis 37	1	6	9
Genesis 41	3	13	13
Exodus 3	7/14	1	14
Exodus 14	12	2	3
Exodus 20	14/7	9	5
Numbers 13	9	8	12
Numbers 14	8	7	2

Person	Place	Event
1. Joseph	Mt. Horeb	Sent here to find a wife for Isaac
2. Lot	Red Sea	Sentenced to wander here for forty years
3. Pharaoh	Eden	Destroyed while pursuing Israelites
4. Jacob	Sodom and Gomorrah	Offered his son in sacrifice
5. Laban	Mt. Ararat	The Ten Commandments were given
6. Servant of Abraham	Dothan	Fled destruction of wicked cities
7. Moses	The wilderness	Deceived by a serpent
8. Children of Israel	Canaan	The ark came to rest
9. Twelve spies	Mt. Sinai	Sold by brothers to Midianites
10. Abraham	Mesopotamia	Wrestled with an angel
11. Eve	Mt. Moriah	Tricked Jacob into marrying older daughter
12. Army of Egypt	Haran	Sent to "search the land" for conquest
13. Noah	Egypt	Had two dreams interpreted by Joseph
14. Moses	Peniel	Called to lead Israel out of Egypt

GET IT TOGETHER #2

Below are listed four groups: Scriptures, Persons, Places, and Events. Your task is to match correctly the person, place, and event from the list below with the Scripture passage on the left side of the chart.

Scripture	Person	Place	Event
Joshua 2			
Joshua 4			
Joshua 6			
Joshua 7			
Joshua 9			
Joshua 10			
Joshua 15			
Judges 3			
Judges 4			
Judges 7			
Judges 14			
Judges 16			

Persons	Places	Events
1. Samson	Kirjathsepher	Caused Israel to lose a battle here
2. A group of kings from Gibeon	An army camp by the Hill of Moreh	Made a riddle about a lion
3. Ehud	Ai	Helped capture a strong man by cutting his hair
4. Gideon and 300 men	Gilgal	Won a battle by marching around a city wall, blowing trumpets and shouting
5. Rahab	Gibeon	Each took a stone to make a memorial
6. Jael	In a summer parlour	Killed a fat king with a dagger
7. Delilah	Jericho	Used pitchers, lamps, and trumpets to win a battle
8. Joshua	The riverbed of Jordan	Hid two spies from Israel
9. Twelve men	Jericho	Tricked Joshua into a peace treaty
10. Five Amorite kings	Plain of Zaanaim by kedesh	Killed a king by driving a tent nail through his head
11. Caleb	Timnath	Defeated by Israel with the help of a hailstorm
12. Achan	Valley of Sorek	Offered his daughter as wife for one who would capture this city

GET IT TOGETHER #2

Below are listed four groups: Scriptures, Persons, Places, and Events. Your task is to match correctly the person, place, and event from the list below with the Scripture passage on the left side of the chart.

Scripture	Person	Place	Event
Joshua 2	5	7/9	8
Joshua 4	9	8	5
Joshua 6	8	7/9	4
Joshua 7	12	3	1
Joshua 9	2	4	9
Joshua 10	10	5	11
Joshua 15	11	1	12
Judges 3	3	6	6
Judges 4	6	10	10
Judges 7	4	2	7
Judges 14	1	11	2
Judges 16	7	12	3

Persons	Places	Events
1. Samson	Kirjathsepher	Caused Israel to lose a battle here
2. A group of kings from Gibeon	An army camp by the Hill of Moreh	Made a riddle about a lion
3. Ehud	Ai	Helped capture a strong man by cutting his hair
4. Gideon and 300 men	Gilgal	Won a battle by marching around a city wall, blowing trumpets and shouting
5. Rahab	Gibeon	Each took a stone to make a memorial
6. Jael	In a summer parlour	Killed a fat king with a dagger
7. Delilah	Jericho	Used pitchers, lamps, and trumpets to win a battle
8. Joshua	The riverbed of Jordan	Hid two spies from Israel
9. Twelve men	Jericho	Tricked Joshua into a peace treaty
10. Five Amorite kings	Plain of Zaanaim by kedesh	Killed a king by driving a tent nail through his head
11. Caleb	Timnath	Defeated by Israel with the help of a hailstorm
12. Achan	Valley of Sorek	Offered his daughter as wife for one who would capture this city

GET IT TOGETHER #3

Below are four groups: Scriptures, Persons, Places, and Events. Your task is to match the person, place, and event from the list below with the passage of the Scripture on the left.

Scripture	Person	Place	Event
2 Kings 17:1-6			
1 Samuel 10:17-24			
1 Kings 8:1-21			
1 Samuel 16:4-13			
2 Kings 18:1-5			
2 Kings 24:10-16			
1 Samuel 13:7-14			
1 Kings 16:29-32			
1 Samuel 17:19-51			
2 Kings 5:1-14			
2 Kings 22:1–23:5			
1 Kings 17:8-16			
1 Kings 22:29-41			
1 Kings 11:43-12:1			

Person	Place	Events
1. Saul	Judah	Samuel anointed Israel's second king
2. Naaman	Bethlehem	This Philistine giant was killed
3. Hezekiah	Zarephath	His army took people of Judah captive
4. Shalmaneser	Assyria	God rejected him as king
5. Jezebel	Gilgal	He presented the first king of Israel
6. Ahab	Samaria	Took Israel there after capture
7. David	Ramoth-gilead	Tore down pagan altars
8. Josiah	Valley of Elah	Slain in battle with Syria
9. Elijah	Jerusalem	Helped Hilkiah renew God's covenant
10. Solomon	Jordan River	King's wife who worshiped Baal
11. Rehoboam	Jerusalem	Fed by a widow
12. Goliath	Mizpeh	Cured of leprosy
13. Nebuchadnezzar	Shechem	Dedicated a new temple to God
14. Samuel	Judah	Crowned king at his father's death

GET IT TOGETHER #3

Below are four groups: Scriptures, Persons, Places, and Events. Your task is to match the person, place, and event from the list below with the passage of the Scripture on the left.

Scripture	Person	Place	Event
2 Kings 17:1-6	4	4	6
1 Samuel 10:17-24	14	12	5
1 Kings 8:1-21	10	9/11	13
1 Samuel 16:4-13	7	2	1
2 Kings 18:1-5	3	1/14	7
2 Kings 24:10-16	13	9/11	3
1 Samuel 13:7-14	1	5	4
1 Kings 16:29-32	5	6	10
1 Samuel 17:19-51	12	8	2
2 Kings 5:1-14	2	10	12
2 Kings 22:1–23:5	8	1/14	9
1 Kings 17:8-16	9	3	11
1 Kings 22:29-41	6	7	8
1 Kings 11:43-12:1	11	13	14

Person	Place	Events
1. Saul	Judah	Samuel anointed Israel's second king
2. Naaman	Bethlehem	This Philistine giant was killed
3. Hezekiah	Zarephath	His army took people of Judah captive
4. Shalmaneser	Assyria	God rejected him as king
5. Jezebel	Gilgal	He presented the first king of Israel
6. Ahab	Samaria	Took Israel there after capture
7. David	Ramoth-gilead	Tore down pagan altars
8. Josiah	Valley of Elah	Slain in battle with Syria
9. Elijah	Jerusalem	Helped Hilkiah renew God's covenant
10. Solomon	Jordan River	King's wife who worshiped Baal
11. Rehoboam	Jerusalem	Fed by a widow
12. Goliath	Mizpeh	Cured of leprosy
13. Nebuchadnezzar	Shechem	Dedicated a new temple to God
14. Samuel	Judah	Crowned king at his father's death

BIBLE PUZZLES

MATCH-IT

3
FILL-IT-IN
VARIETY PUZZLES

1. JOHN
2. TITUS
3. JUDE
4. ROMANS
5. JAMES
6. PHILEMON
7. ACTS
8. MARK
9. LUKE
10. GALATIANS
11. HEBREWS
12. SECOND CORINTHIANS
13. EPHESIANS
14. SECOND JOHN
15. FIRST PETER
16. FIRST TIMOTHY
17. MATTHEW
18. COLOSSIANS
19. FIRST JOHN
20. SECOND TIMOTHY
21. REVELATION
22. FIRST CORINTHIANS
23. PHILIPPIANS
24. FIRST THESSALONIANS
25. SECOND PETER
26. SECOND THESSALONIANS
27. THIRD JOHN

OLD TESTAMENT BIBLE CHAIN

Decide which Bible book answers each chain. Put the letter after the chain in the box above the book's name. Read the message spelled out.

Isaiah + 6 books	= P
Jonah – 4 books	= R
Proverbs – 5 books	= A
Ezekiel + 10 books	= O
Daniel – 4 books	= '
2 Kings + 15 books	= S
Amos – 12 books	= W
Ruth + 9 books	= S
Jeremiah + 8 books	= N
Ezra – 6 books	= V
Micah + 4 books	= D
Joel + 5 books	= A
Numbers + 7 books	= E
Ezra – 2 books	= C
Job + 10 books – 2 books	= E
Exodus + 7 books – 2 books	= O
Psalms + 8 books – 3 books	= G

Jeremiah	Judges	Haggai	Isaiah	Esther	Joel	Zephaniah	Job	1 Kings	Hosea	1 Chronicles	Ezra	Jonah	Daniel	Nahum	1 Samuel	Ezekiel

OLD TESTAMENT BIBLE CHAIN

Decide which Bible book answers each chain. Put the letter after the chain in the box above the book's name. Read the message spelled out.

Isaiah + 6 books	=P
Jonah − 4 books	= R
Proverbs − 5 books	= A
Ezekiel + 10 books	= O
Daniel − 4 books	= '
2 Kings + 15 books	= S
Amos − 12 books	= W
Ruth + 9 books	= S
Jeremiah + 8 books	= N
Ezra − 6 books	= V
Micah + 4 books	= D
Joel + 5 books	= A
Numbers + 7 books	= E
Ezra − 2 books	= C
Job + 10 books − 2 books	= E
Exodus + 7 books − 2 books	= O
Psalms + 8 books − 3 books	= G

G	O	D	'	S	P	O	W	E	R	C	A	N	S	A	V	E
Jeremiah	Judges	Haggai	Isaiah	Esther	Joel	Zephaniah	Job	1 Kings	Hosea	1 Chronicles	Ezra	Jonah	Daniel	Nahum	1 Samuel	Ezekiel

NEW TESTAMENT BIBLE CHAIN

Put the letter after the chain in the box above the answer below.

Luke + 8 books	= H
Titus + 6 books	= N
Romans − 4 books	= N
James − 10 books	= E
Galatians + 10 books	= E
Acts + 7 books − 3 books	= I
1 Timothy + 5 books	= E
Ephesians − 7 books	= L
Mark + 20 books	= S
Colossians − 7 books	= T
1 Peter + 5 books − 8 books	= T
John + 13 books	= H
Jude − 14 books	= S
Hebrews + 8 books	= O

Luke	Hebrews	Acts	Philemon	Philippians	James	2 Peter	Revelation	Mark	Colossians	Titus	Galatians	1 John	Ephesians

NEW TESTAMENT BIBLE CHAIN

Put the letter after the chain in the box above the answer below.

Luke + 8 books	= H
Titus + 6 books	= N
Romans − 4 books	= N
James − 10 books	= E
Galatians + 10 books	= E
Acts + 7 books − 3 books	= I
1 Timothy + 5 books	= E
Ephesians − 7 books	= L
Mark + 20 books	= S
Colossians − 7 books	= T
1 Peter + 5 books − 8 books	= T
John + 13 books	= H
Jude − 14 books	= S
Hebrews + 8 books	= O

L	E	T	T	H	E	S	O	N	S	H	I	N	E
Luke	Hebrews	Acts	Philemon	Philippians	James	2 Peter	Revelation	Mark	Colossians	Titus	Galatians	1 John	Ephesians

MISSING CONSONANTS—OLD TESTAMENT

Below are the Old Testament books with the consonants missing. See if you can figure them out by supplying the missing letters.

1. _ E P _ A _ I A _
2. O _ A _ I A _
3. _ E _ I _ I _ U _
4. _ I _ _ _ _ _ I _ _ _
5. _ E _ O _ _ _ A _ U E _
6. _ E U _ E _ O _ O _ Y
7. E _ _ _ _ E _ I A _ _ E _
8. _ U _ _ E _ _
9. _ A _ A _ _ I
10. _ _ O _ E _ _ _
11. N E _ E _ I A _
12. _ A _ E _ _ A _ I O _ _ _
13. _ E C _ A _ I A _
14. _ A _ A _ _ U _
15. _ E _ O _ _ _ I _ _ _
16. _ E _ E _ I A _
17. _ _ A _ _ _
18. _ I _ _ _ _ _ A _ U E _
19. _ E _ O _ _ _ _ _ _ O _ I _ _ E _
20. _ O _ _ O _ _ O _ O _ O _
21. _ I _ _ _ _ _ _ O _ I _ _ E _

22. _ A _ _ A I
23. _ O E _
24. _ I _ A _
25. _ A _ I E _
26. _ O _ A _
27. _ A _ U _
28. _ U _ _
29. E _ _ A
30. _ O _ E A
31. A _ O _
32. E _ _ _ E _
33. _ O _
34. E _ O _ U _
35. I _ A I A _
36. _ U _ _ E _
37. _ O _ _ U A
38. E _ E _ I E _
39. _ E _ E _ I _

51

MISSING CONSONANTS—OLD TESTAMENT

Below are the Old Testament books with the consonants missing. See if you can figure them out by supplying the missing letters.

1. ZEPHANIAH
2. OBADIAH
3. LEVITICUS
4. FIRST KINGS
5. SECOND SAMUEL
6. DEUTERONOMY
7. ECCLESIASTES
8. NUMBERS
9. MALACHI
10. PROVERBS
11. NEHEMIAH
12. LAMENTATIONS
13. ZECHARIAH
14. HABAKKUK
15. SECOND KINGS
16. JEREMIAH
17. PSALMS
18. FIRST SAMUEL

22. HAGGAI
23. JOEL
24. MICAH
25. DANIEL
26. JONAH
27. NAHUM
28. RUTH
29. EZRA
30. HOSEA
31. AMOS
32. ESTHER
33. JOB
34. EXODUS
35. ISAIAH
36. JUDGES
37. JOSHUA
38. EZEKIEL
39. GENESIS

19. SECOND CHRONICLES
20. SONG OF SOLOMON
21. FIRST CHRONICLES

MISSING CONSONANTS—NEW TESTAMENT

Below are the New Testament books with the consonants missing. See if you can figure them out by supplying the missing letters.

1. __ O __ __
2. __ I __ U __
3. __ __ D E
4. __ O __ A __ __
5. __ A __ E __
6. __ __ I __ E __ O __
7. A __ __ __ __
8. __ A __ __ __
9. __ U __ E
10. __ A __ A __ I A __ __
11. __ E __ __ E __ __
12. __ E __ O __ __ __ O __ I __ __ __ I A __ __
13. E __ __ E __ I A __ __
14. __ E __ O __ __ __ O __ __
15. __ I __ __ __ __ E __ E __
16. __ I __ __ __ __ __ I __ O __ __ Y
17. __ A __ __ __ E __
18. __ O __ O __ __ I A __ __ __
19. __ I __ __ __ __ O __ __
20. __ E __ O __ __ __ I __ O __ __ Y
21. __ E __ E __ A __ I O __
22. __ I __ __ __ __ O __ I __ __ __ I A __ __
23. __ __ I __ I __ __ I A __ __
24. __ I __ __ __ __ __ E __ __ A __ O __ I A __ __
25. __ E __ O __ __ __ E __ E __
26. __ E __ O __ __ __ __ E __ __ A __ O __ I A __ __ __
27. __ __ I __ __ __ O __ __

53

MISSING CONSONANTS—NEW TESTAMENT

Below are the New Testament books with the consonants missing. See if you can figure them out by supplying the missing letters.

1. J O H N
2. T I T U S
3. J U D E
4. R O M A N S
5. J A M E S
6. P H I L E M O N
7. A C T S
8. M A R K
9. L U K E
10. G A L A T I A N S
11. H E B R E W S
12. S E C O N D C O R I N T H I A N S
13. E P H E S I A N S
14. S E C O N D J O H N
15. F I R S T P E T E R
16. F I R S T T I M O T H Y
17. M A T T H E W
18. C O L O S S I A N S
19. F I R S T J O H N
20. S E C O N D T I M O T H Y
21. R E V E L A T I O N
22. F I R S T C O R I N T H I A N S
23. P H I L I P P I A N S
24. F I R S T T H E S S A L O N I A N S
25. S E C O N D P E T E R
26. S E C O N D T H E S S A L O N I A N S
27. T H I R D J O H N

UNSCRAMBLE THESE OLD TESTAMENT BOOKS

1. ELOJ _ _ _ _

2. THRU _ _ _ _ _

3. ANJOH _ _ _ _ _ _

4. EADNIL _ _ _ _ _ _ _

5. IAHSAI _ _ _ _ _ _

6. GEJSUD _ _ _ _ _ _

7. MSLPSA _ _ _ _ _ _

8. MNAUH _ _ _ _ _ _

9. RZEA _ _ _ _

10. GIKNS _ _ _ _ _ _

11. AHCIM _ _ _ _ _

12. AGIGHA _ _ _ _ _ _

13. MASEUL _ _ _ _ _ _

14. HUASOJ _ _ _ _ _ _

15. OJB _ _ _

16. MOAS _ _ _ _

17. STEEHR _ _ _ _ _ _ _

18. OSEAH _ _ _ _ _

19. BNUMSRE _ _ _ _ _ _ _

20. NEGSIES _ _ _ _ _ _ _

21. DIHAAOB _ _ _ _ _ _ _

22. UKHKAKBA _ _ _ _ _ _ _ _

23. DOUSXE _ _ _ _ _ _

24. HAPEZHAIN _ _ _ _ _ _ _ _ _

25. BROPVSER _ _ _ _ _ _ _ _

26. ZEKEELI _ _ _ _ _ _ _

27. NORICHCESL _ _ _ _ _ _ _ _ _ _

28. ITCSUVLEI _ _ _ _ _ _ _ _ _

29. HACIAML _ _ _ _ _ _ _

30. HARZECIAH _ _ _ _ _ _ _ _ _

31. HEMNEHAI _ _ _ _ _ _ _ _

32. REMEJAIH _ _ _ _ _ _ _ _

33. GNOSFOMONOLOS _ _ _ _ _ _ _ _ _ _ _ _ _

34. TESCECLEISAS _ _ _ _ _ _ _ _ _ _ _ _

35. RETONUEDMYO _ _ _ _ _ _ _ _ _ _ _

36. TENMALATINOS _ _ _ _ _ _ _ _ _ _ _ _

UNSCRAMBLE THESE OLD TESTAMENT BOOKS

1. ELOJ JOEL
2. THRU RUTH
3. ANJOH JONAH
4. EADNIL DANIEL
5. IAHSAI ISAIAH
6. GEJSUD JUDGES
7. MSLPSA PSALMS
8. MNAUH NAHUM
9. RZEA EZRA
10. GIKNS KINGS
11. AHCIM MICAH
12. AGIGHA HAGGAI
13. MASEUL SAMUEL
14. HUASOJ JOSHUA
15. OJB JOB
16. MOAS AMOS

17. STEEHR ESTHER
18. OSEAH HOSEA
19. BNUMSRE NUMBERS
20. NEGSIES GENESIS
21. DIHAAOB OBADIAH
22. UKHKAKBA HABAKKUK
23. DOUSXE EXODUS
24. HAPEZHAIN ZEPHANIAH
25. BROPVSER PROVERBS
26. ZEKEELI EZEKIEL
27. NORICHCESL CHRONICLES
28. ITCSUVLEI LEVITICUS
29. HACIAML MALACHI
30. HARZECIAH ZECHARIAH
31. HEMNEHAI NEHEMIAH
32. REMEJAIH JEREMIAH

33. GNOSFOMONOLOS SONG OF SOLOMON
34. TESCECLEISAS ECCLESIASTES
35. RETONUEDMYO DEUTERONOMY
36. TENMALATINOS LAMENTATIONS

UNSCRAMBLE THESE NEW TESTAMENT BOOKS

Write the name of the New Testament book under each scrambled word.

1. TMOITYH
   _ _ _ _ _ _ _

2. TEPRE
   _ _ _ _ _

3. TTHAMWE
   _ _ _ _ _ _ _

4. CTAS
   _ _ _ _

5. MEAJS
   _ _ _ _ _

6. DJEU
   _ _ _ _

7. OJNH
   _ _ _ _

8. KARM
   _ _ _ _

9. KULE
   _ _ _ _

10. TUITS
    _ _ _ _ _

11. HEISNASEP
    _ _ _ _ _ _ _ _ _

12. MOANRS
    _ _ _ _ _ _

13. THISANINCRO
    _ _ _ _ _ _ _ _ _ _ _

14. TAAALGNIS
    _ _ _ _ _ _ _ _ _

15. LATEVERNOI
    _ _ _ _ _ _ _ _ _ _

16. LEMONIHP
    _ _ _ _ _ _ _ _

17. BREWSHE
    _ _ _ _ _ _ _

18. HESSSTANAINOL
    _ _ _ _ _ _ _ _ _ _ _ _ _

19. HPIANPLIPSI
    _ _ _ _ _ _ _ _ _ _ _

20. LOOCSISASN
    _ _ _ _ _ _ _ _ _ _

FIND SOME HIDDEN BOOKS IN THESE SENTENCES.

The names of New Testament books are found in the sentences below. Underline the letters that spell out each book.

1. Here are the facts.

2. Buy that small ukelele.

3. She brews a good cup of tea.

4. We like grape jam especially well.

5. Is this a markdown sale?

6. I met my cousin Hiram at the well.

7. After playing the trumpet, Eric sat down.

8. I am Arkansas bound tonight.

UNSCRAMBLE THESE NEW TESTAMENT BOOKS

Write the name of the New Testament book under each scrambled word.

1. TMOITYH
   TIMOTHY

2. TEPRE
   PETER

3. TTHAMWE
   MATTHEW

4. CTAS
   ACTS

5. MEAJS
   JAMES

6. DJEU
   JUDE

7. OJNH
   JOHN

8. KARM
   MARK

9. KULE
   LUKE

10. TUITS
    TITUS

11. HEISNASEP
    EPHESIANS

12. MOANRS
    ROMANS

13. THISANINCRO
    CORINTHIANS

14. TAAALGNIS
    GALATIANS

15. LATEVERNOI
    REVELATION

16. LEMONIHP
    PHILEMON

17. BREWSHE
    HEBREWS

18. HESSSTANAINOL
    THESSALONIANS

19. HPIANPLIPSI
    PHILIPPIANS

20. LOOCSISASN
    COLOSSIANS

FIND SOME HIDDEN BOOKS IN THESE SENTENCES

The names of New Testament books are found in the sentences below Underline the letters that spell out each book.

1. Here are the facts.

2. Buy that small ukelele.

3. She brews a good cup of tea.

4. We like grape jam especially well.

5. Is this a markdown sale?

6. I met my cousin Hiram at the well.

7. After playing the trumpet, Eric sat down.

8. I am Arkansas bound tonight.

HIDDEN BIBLE BOOKS

Twenty-nine books of the Bible are hidden in this story. See how many you can find. Example: Donna hummed.

A TRIP TO AI

I went to visit my cousin Donna in the city Ai last week. As Donna hummed, I asked her, "Is this Ai a holy city?" She said that it wasn't and silently pointed to the letter "J" on a high cliff. A "J", oh now I knew why everyone was so frightened. Ai was ruled by a wicked chief named Jezebel.

As I turned around, I saw a sedan coming down the street driven by Philipp. As I approached the sedan, I elbowed by several people in order to speak with the driver. Someone asked me the driver's name. "Philipp," I answered. His job was to drive the chief of the city wherever she wanted to go. The passenger inside was as dismal a chief as I had ever seen. She was wearing blue hose and the brew she was drinking was green in color.

From answers I got from Philipp, I found out that she always acts strange and that he was thinking of quitting. He said that the old hag gained the office by committing dishonest deeds. She even has her pet ermine living in the palace. Whenever she sees anyone with money, she pumps alms from them saying that it's for the poor. The last time she got some alms money, she bought an oil well, a banjo, elephant, a Moses picture, an encyclopedia set and a giraffe. If she hears anyone mocking, she sends them to jail. When Philipp's brother Jud expressed his feelings about her, she sent him to the prison across the street. Jud gestured to me as we passed.

I told Philipp I had better be getting on my way to meet my wife. "Where is your gal at?" I answered Philipp by explaining that she was to meet me at the well.

"I am at the well every day from noon to three if you wish to visit again."

I went on toward the well and I saw as comic a hat as I had ever seen. I felt like I was getting the flu and began to walk slower. The flu kept me from getting to the well sooner than I did. My wife had bought a jar of jam especially for me, and also a long silver object. It was a bit; it usually goes in a camel's mouth.

My wife asked if I wanted to buy a camel's hair coat this year. "Not I, moth, you know, eats camel hair," I answered. I then told my wife we were getting in a rut here, and I had decided we should go home.

My wife replied, "Too bad, I a home in Ai had planned."

HIDDEN BIBLE BOOKS

Twenty-nine books of the Bible are hidden in this story. See how many you can find. Example: Donna hummed.

A TRIP TO AI

I went to visit my cousin Donna in the city Ai last week. As Donna hummed, I asked her, "Is this Ai a holy city?" She said that it wasn't and silently pointed to the letter "J" on a high cliff. A "J", oh now I knew why everyone was so frightened. Ai was ruled by a wicked chief named Jezebel.

As I turned around, I saw a sedan coming down the street driven by Philipp. As I approached the sedan, I elbowed by several people in order to speak with the driver. Someone asked me the driver's name. "Philipp," I answered. His job was to drive the chief of the city wherever she wanted to go. The passenger inside was as dismal a chief as I had ever seen. She was wearing blue hose and the brew she was drinking was green in color.

From answers I got from Philipp, I found out that she always acts strange and that he was thinking of quitting. He said that the old hag gained the office by committing dishonest deeds. She even has her pet ermine living in the palace. Whenever she sees anyone with money, she pumps alms from them saying that it's for the poor. The last time she got some alms money, she bought an oil well, a banjo, elephant, a Moses picture, an encyclopedia set and a giraffe. If she hears anyone mocking, she sends them to jail. When Philipp's brother Jud expressed his feelings about her, she sent him to the prison across the street. Jud gestured to me as we passed.

I told Philipp I had better be getting on my way to meet my wife. "Where is your gal at?" I answered Philipp by explaining that she was to meet me at the well.

"I am at the well every day from noon to three if you wish to visit again."

I went on toward the well and I saw as comic a hat as I had ever seen. I felt like I was getting the flu and began to walk slower. The flu kept me from getting to the well sooner than I did. My wife had bought a jar of jam especially for me, and also a long silver object. It was a bit; it usually goes in a camel's mouth.

My wife asked if I wanted to buy a camel's hair coat this year. "Not I, moth, you know, eats camel hair," I answered. I then told my wife we were getting in a rut here, and I had decided we should go home.

My wife replied, "Too bad, I a home in Ai had planned."

BIBLE TIC-TAC-TOE

A team game. Player whose turn it is selects a topic. If he answers the question correctly, his team marks the box with an X or an O. If he misses, the other team gets a chance to answer the same question.

Old Testament Books	Bible Cities	New Testament Books
New Testament Men	Miracles	Old Testament Men
Parables	Bible Numbers	Bible Women

Sample Questions:

Old Testament Books	Bible Cities	New Testament Books	New Testament Men	Miracles
1. Name the sixth book. 2. Name the book about the conquest. 3. Name the book after Ezra. 4. Where do we read about David? 5. Name the book about Creation. 6. What book has the Ten Commandments?	1. Where was Jesus born? 2. Where did Jesus live as a boy? 3. Where was Paul going to persecute Christians? 4. Where Peter first preached. 5. Where Paul was from. 6. Where Paul was stoned.	1. Name the book after Romans. 2. Name a book written by Paul. 3. Name a book telling of Jesus. 4. Name the shortest book. 5. Name the book before Titus. 6. How many books are in the New Testament?	1. Name the father of John the Baptist. 2. Name a companion of Paul in prison. 3. Who denied Christ? 4. Who betrayed Christ? 5. Who doubted Christ? 6. Who was king at Jesus' birth?	1. What was used to feed 5,000? 2. How did the Israelites cross the Jordan River? 3. What happened to Lot's wife? 4. Who healed ten lepers? 5. What miracle involved Naaman? 6. Who was not killed by a snake bite?

Old Testament Men	Parables	Numbers	Bible Women
1. Name the strong man of the Old Testament. 2. Name the first murderer. 3. Who was sold by his brothers? 4. Who was put in a den of lions? 5. Name the sons of Noah. 6. Who received the old law?	1. Who helped a beaten man? 2. Why were some virgins foolish? 3. Where did the wise man build? 4. Where did the seed fall? 5. Name three things that were lost. 6. Tell about the rich man.	1. Number of days it rained on Noah. 2. Times Peter denied Christ. 3. Number of Noah's sons. 4. Number of Joseph's brothers. 5. Number of Jacob's wives. 6. Number of Paul's journeys.	1. Name the first woman. 2. Name the wife of Abraham. 3. Who betrayed Samson? 4. Name the mother of John the Baptist. 5. Who helped the spies in Jericho? 6. Name the mother of Jesus.

BIBLE
TIC-TAC-TOE

Answers to Sample Questions

Old Testament Books

1. Joshua
2. Joshua
3. Nehemiah
4. I & 2 Samuel, I Chronicles
5. Genesis
6. Exodus, Deuteronomy

New Testament Men

1. Zacharias
2. Silas
3. Peter
4. Judas Iscariot
5. Thomas
6. Herod

Parables

1. Good Samaritan
2. Didn't bring oil for lamps
3. On a rock
4. On the wayside, stony places, among thorns and on good ground
5. Sheep, coin, son
6. In Hell he saw Lazarus with Abraham

Bible Cities

1. Bethlehem
2. Nazareth
3. Damascus
4. Jerusalem
5. Tarsus
6. Lystra

Miracles

1. 5 loaves, 2 fish
2. The water stopped flowing as soon as the priests entered the water.
3. She turned into a pillar of salt.
4. Jesus
5. Healed of leprosy
6. Paul

Numbers

1. 40
2. 3
3. 3
4. 11
5. 4
6. 3 (and 1 to Rome)

New Testament Books

1. I Corinthians
2. (Various answers)
3. (Any of 1st four books)
4. 2 John
5. 2 Timothy
6. 27

Old Testament Men

1. Samson
2. Cain
3. Joseph
4. Daniel
5. Shem, Ham, Japheth
6. Moses

Bible Women

1. Eve
2. Sarah
3. Delilah
4. Elisabeth
5. Rahab
6. Mary